Grade K

Interim Assessments

BENCHMARK EDUCATION COMPANY

Benchmark Education Company
145 Huguenot Street • New Rochelle, NY 10801

Senior Project Editor: Sherine Gilmour
Assistant Editor: Nicholas DeLibero
Creative Director: Laurie Berger
Designer: Sophia Oliboni
Director of Photography: Doug Schneider
Photo Assistant: Jackie Friedman
Illustrations: Marcela Gomez

Printed in Guangzhou, China. 4401/0319/CA21900194
ISBN: 978-1-5125-5195-2

Interim Assessments

Table of Contents

Overview

The *Benchmark Advance* core literacy program has ten units per grade in Grades K–6. Each three-week unit focuses on a unit concept, such as "Technology and Society" or "Point of View," and a grade-appropriate topic. Each unit provides reading selections related to the topic. Most units focus on informational or literary genres, although some units offer both. Instruction in each unit focuses on reading comprehension and vocabulary, reading foundational skills (in Grades K–2) or word study, and writing.

This book provides a set of Interim Assessments and Performance Tasks designed to assess students' progress in reading and writing, based on the standards and skills taught across the units. Both types of assessment are aligned to the Common Core State Standards for each grade level. Descriptions of the Interim Assessments and the Performance Tasks are provided in the following sections, along with directions for administering and scoring the assessments, and directions for interpreting scores.

Description of Assessments

Benchmark Advance offers an array of assessments to inform and support the instructional program. In keeping with the Common Core State Standards and the best current assessment practices, Benchmark assessments use a variety of item types, as described below.

Item Types:

All of the reading questions in the Interim Assessments are selected-response items. The Grades K–1 assessments all use multiple-choice items with three answer choices. (Grade K answers are pictures, not text.) In Grades 2–6, there are several different item types, as described below. (The "nontraditional" and technology-enhanced items make up about 20 to 30 percent of each assessment.)*

- A multiple-choice item provides three or four answer choices, depending on grade level. Students choose one correct answer.

- A multiple-response item provides more than four answer choices labeled by letters (A, B, C, . . .). Students choose two or three correct answers. Each answer is worth 1 point.

- A two-part item consists of Part A and Part B. In general, the first part is a multiple-choice item that asks a question with one correct answer; the second part asks students to find evidence from the passage to support the answer in Part A. The second part may have more than one correct response.

- An "inline choice" item presents a drop-down menu of answer choices to complete a sentence. There is only one correct answer from each menu.

- Students answer some questions by selecting checkboxes or highlighting words, phrases, or sentences in the excerpt.

- Some items involve checkboxes in a table (to indicate Yes/No, Fact/Opinion, etc.).

- For some questions, students choose the answers and write them in (or drag-and-drop them into) the correct boxes.

In these types of items, each correct response is generally worth 1 point. Some items with multiple responses are scored with 2-point rubrics instead.

*Please note that technology-enhanced item types are designed for online testing. The formats and directions have been adapted from the print version.

The Grade 2–6 assessments also include two other types of items:

- The Performance Tasks include constructed-response items. This kind of item presents a question or short-answer prompt. Students respond by writing a response of two to four sentences. This type of item is scored using a 2-point scoring rubric. Students may earn 0, 1, or 2 points for a response.

- Both the Interim Assessments and the Performance Tasks include writing prompts. A writing prompt poses a question or gives a direction. Students respond by writing an extended response, such as a report, essay, opinion, or narrative. The writing prompt is scored using a 4-point scoring rubric. Students may earn 0, 1, 2, 3, or 4 points for a response. (Teachers have an option of scoring the writing a second time for conventions and grammar, using a different 4-point rubric.).

These two kinds of items are scored by hand.

Interim Assessments

In Grades K–6, students take four Interim Assessments per grade based on the Common Core State Standards taught throughout the year. These assessments are intended to help teachers monitor student progress and provide summative information—essentially, to see if students are making adequate progress and staying on track. Information from these assessments can help teachers plan instruction for upcoming units.

In each grade, Interim Assessment 1 is taken twice: once at the beginning of the year as a pretest and then again as a posttest. Its purpose is twofold: (1) to help determine where students are in relation to grade-level expectations and (2) to establish a baseline for measuring each student's progress.

Interim Assessment 2 is based on the standards taught in Units 1–3; it is intended to be administered upon completion of Unit 3. Interim Assessment 3 is based on the standards taught in Units 1–6; it is intended to be administered upon completion of Unit 6.

Interim Assessment 1 is intended to be administered at the beginning and again at the end of the year, or upon completion of Unit 10, as a posttest. This is designed to allow for direct comparison of student performance between assessments 1 and 4. This kind of information, from the beginning of the year to the end, can be used to determine how much progress students have made during the course of the school year.

The Interim Assessments include informational and literary reading passages; a set of test questions/items that assesses comprehension, vocabulary, and reading foundational skills (in Grades K–2) or word study; and a writing prompt (Grades 1–6). In all grades, the questions for comprehension, vocabulary, and word study are integrated with the reading passages. In Grades K–2, questions testing reading foundational skills are provided in a separate subtest. The number of reading passages and items in the assessments vary by grade, as shown in the table below.

Number of Passages and Items Per Assessment						
Grade	Passage	Reading Comp	Vocabulary	RF Skills / Word Study	Total Points	Writing
K	2	10	5	15	30	N/A
1	2	10	5	15	30	1
2	3	15	5	15	35	1
3	3	20	6	9	35	1
4	4	26	8	6	40	1
5	4	26	8	6	40	1
6	4	26	8	6	40	1

Note: As explained above, these assessments use different types of items. Some items have one correct answer; some have more than one correct answer. Each correct response is worth 1 point. The number of items in the table is actually the number of points. For example, Interim Assessment 1 in Grade 4 has 40 questions/items, worth a total of 40 points. The number of points per test stays the same in each grade; the number of questions may vary.

The chart below shows the approximate passage length and Lexile range for passages in the Interim Assessments, Grades 1–6. The length may vary in some cases where paired passages are used or text features, such as sidebars, are included. Note that the Kindergarten passages are read aloud to the students, not by the students. The Grade 1 passages are read aloud and the students read along.

Reading Passages in the Interim Assessments				
Grade	Assessments 1 and 4 Lexile Range	Assessment 2 Lexile Range	Assessment 3 Lexile Range	Passage Length
1	180–280	180–220	220–310	100–200 words
2	350–480	350–430	430–500	200–300 words
3	500–650	500–590	590–680	250–400 words
4	600–730	600–680	680–750	300–450 words
5	800–900	800–860	860–920	300–500 words
6	900–980	900–950	950–990	300–600 words

How to Administer the Interim Assessments

For Grades K–6, the chart below shows the estimated time for administering the Interim Assessments.

Estimated Times for Administration (in Minutes)			
Grade	Reading	RF Skills	Writing
K	20–25	15–20	N/A
1	20–25	15–20	15–20
2	25–30	15–20	20–25
3	45–50		30–40
4	50–60		30–40
5	50–60		30–40
6	50–60		30–40

The Interim Assessments may be administered in two or more sittings. In Grades 1 and 2, for example, the three parts of the test could be administered in three separate sessions. In Grades 3–6, the Reading section could be administered in one sitting and the Writing Prompt in another. If necessary, the Reading section may be administered in two parts by having students read the first passage(s) and answering the associated questions.

These time allowances are for planning purposes only. These assessments are not intended to be timed; students should be allowed more time if needed.

Directions for Administering an Interim Assessment

1. Make a copy of the assessment for each student.

2. Have students write their name and the date at the top of the first page.

3. Read aloud the directions at the top of the first page.

   Note: In Grade 1, Interim Assessments 1 (pretest) and 2 are designed to have the teacher read the passages and questions aloud. For Interim Assessments 3 and 4 (posttest), students are expected to read the passages and questions themselves. All of the questions in Grades K–1 are multiple-choice with three answer choices.

4. For multiple-choice questions, tell students to choose the best answer to each question and circle the letter of the correct response (A, B, or C in Grades 1–2; A, B, C, or D in Grades 3–6).

5. For other types of items, students should read and follow the directions carefully, especially when choosing more than one answer to a question. (The number of answers required is always printed in bold type in the question or the directions.) Since these item types may be new to some students, the students may need a little help in understanding how to respond to the questions—at least in the first few assessments until they have had some practice with different types of questions.

6. In Grades 2–6, some multiple-choice items have two parts, labeled Part A and Part B. In general, Part A asks a question about the passage and Part B asks students to find evidence to support the answer in Part A. Have students answer Part A first and then Part B.

7. To administer the Writing Prompt, you may want to administer the test in two parts—the reading section and the writing prompt—with a break in between. Have students read the prompt and then write on the lined pages in the test or on separate pieces of paper. Each writing prompt is worth 4 points. Student responses will be evaluated by rubric; students may receive 0 to 4 points for a written essay or composition.

8. Monitor students as they work on the assessment to make sure they are following directions and know what to do.

9. When students have finished, collect the assessments.

How to Score the Interim Assessments

1. Make a copy of the Interim Assessment Scoring Chart for each student (or you may choose to mark all scores on the test itself). Charts are found at the end of the Answer Key.

2. Refer to the Answer Key for the Interim Assessment. It gives the correct response(s) for each question. A correct response may be a letter (A, B, C . . .), a word or phrase, or a sentence, depending on the type of item.

   For each question, compare each of the student's answers with the Answer Key. If the student's answer is correct, put a check mark (a) beside the item number. If the item has more than one correct answer, make a check mark (a) for each correct answer. If it is incorrect (or blank), cross out the item number with an X.

   Note: In a few cases, you will find a 2-point scoring rubric with criteria for correct responses. Follow the rubric to determine whether the student's response should get zero, one, or two check marks.

3. For two-part items, follow the same procedure with each part. The parts may be scored as separate items. However, the student must get the answer to Part A correct in order to get credit for a correct answer in Part B. (The two parts are closely related; Part B gives evidence for the correct answer in Part A, so the answers to both parts must correspond.) Students may get credit for Part A regardless of how they answer Part B, but they may not get credit for Part B only.

4. To find the total test score, add the number of correct responses (check marks). To find the percent score, use this formula:

   Number correct (points) ÷ total number of points x 100 = %

   For example, the Grade 2 test has a total of 35 points in the Reading section. A student who gets 28 correct answers (28 points) has a percent score of 28/35 = 0.8 x 100 = 80%.

   Use the Interim Assessment Scoring Chart to record each student's score on one assessment. Use the Interim Assessment Progress Class Chart to record scores for all students on all Interim Assessments administered during the school year.

Using the Assessment Results

On an Interim Assessment, the student's score will help indicate the student's progress, based on the standards and skills taught during the school year. A score of 90–100 percent correct is excellent; 80–89 percent is good; 70–79 percent is proficient. Anything below 70 percent may merit further analysis.

However, the main purpose of these assessments is to monitor progress. When evaluating test scores, look for steady progress from the beginning of the year to the end. For a student who scores below 80 percent on Interim Assessment 1, scores may be expected to rise 5–10 percent in each quarter. Students who score above 80 percent on Interim Assessment 1 may show less progress (because there is less room for improvement from 80–100 percent) but should still be expected to demonstrate steady growth. Especially at early grades, students develop reading and writing skills at widely varying rates. Student progress should be evaluated with this factor in mind.

Information from an Interim Assessment, especially Assessment 1 (pretest), may be used in a general way to help plan instruction for upcoming units. For example, a student might score well on vocabulary and word study questions but not in comprehension. This kind of information can be helpful in deciding what to emphasize in the instructional plans for different students.

For a more detailed analysis of a student's score, you may refer to the Answer Key. For each item, the Answer Key indicates the Common Core State Standard. The standard indicates whether an item tests informational (RI) or literary (RL) skills, language (L), reading foundational (RF) skills, or writing (W). (In Grades K–2, RF skill items are listed in separate subtests.) You may gather more detailed information about a student's test score by comparing the student's answers to the Answer Key. This approach can be used to get a general sense of how students performed in different areas.

However, item-by-item scores should be interpreted cautiously because some standards may be tested by only one or two items, and that is not enough to justify any conclusions about specific skills. We recommend looking at Interim Assessment scores for the total test as indications of progress and information to be used for summative assessment decisions, such as determining overall grades.

Reviewing a student's assessment with the student may also be helpful. It can provide an opportunity for students to see which questions they answered incorrectly and why their answers were incorrect. This kind of review will help them be more successful next time.

Performance Tasks

The *Benchmark Advance* literacy program provides Performance Tasks for Grades 2–6. These tasks are assessments based on the Common Core State Standards and the kinds of tasks required of students who take the Smarter Balanced Assessments.

The tasks in this book can be used as medium-cycle assessments for both formative and summative purposes. Once a student has completed the designated units, the Performance Task can serve as a summative assessment of what the student has learned thus far, and as a formative assessment that can direct instruction for the following units.

The assessment component for each grade offers three Performance Tasks: one literary task and two informational tasks. Each task has two parts. Part 1 presents two or three sources (reading passages or videos) for students to read or view and a set of six selected-response and constructed-response questions. Part 2 provides a writing prompt.

In each grade, the three tasks include the following:

- The literary task is intended to be administered after Unit 2. It provides two literary passages (or three, if one is short, such as a poem) for students to read. The questions assess Reading Literature (RL) standards, and the writing task requires narrative writing.

- One informational task is intended to be administered after Unit 5. It provides one or two informational passages for students to read and a short video for students to view. The questions assess Reading for Information (RI) standards, and the writing task requires an opinion or argument.

- One informational task is intended to be administered after Unit 8. It provides one or two informational passages for students to read and Grades 4 and 5 have a short video for students to view. The questions assess Reading for Information (RI) standards, and the writing task requires informative writing.

In each task, the selected-response and constructed-response questions require critical thinking about the source materials. Most of the selected-response items in these assessments have two parts. Part A asks a question, and Part B asks the student to find evidence to support the answer in Part A. Some items are multiple-response questions; the student must choose two answers. Constructed-response items require a written response of two to four sentences. These questions are designed to help students think about the sources in ways that will help prepare them for the final writing task. The writing prompt then asks students to write an extended response based on the information provided in the sources.

How to Administer a Performance Task

This book includes teacher directions and student directions for each Performance Task. Each task is organized in two parts, and each part takes 30–40 minutes to administer. You may plan to have students complete both parts of the task in one day with a break between sessions, or you may administer the two parts on different days.

1. To administer a Performance Task, make a copy of the task for each student.

2. When students are ready to begin, have them read the directions for Part 1. Or you may read the directions aloud as students follow along. Answer any questions that students may have.

3. For Part 1 of the task, have students read each passage (or watch the video, if applicable) and answer the questions. Students should mark and write their answers to the question on the pages. Collect all materials after students have completed this first part.

4. For Part 2 of the task, return materials to the students and have them respond to the writing prompt. Students can write and revise their writing piece on their own paper. Students may review their answers from Part 1 but may not change them at this time.

5. When students have finished Part 2, collect all materials.

How to Score a Performance Task

The scoring of a Performance Task involves scoring the selected-response questions, scoring the constructed-response questions, and scoring the student's written composition. Refer to the Answer Key for the Performance Task you are scoring.

1. To score the selected-response questions, compare the student's answers with the correct responses listed in the Answer Key. Each selected-response question has two correct answers. For all two-part items, Part A is worth 1 point. If Part A is answered correctly, then Part B is worth 1 additional point. If the answer to Part A is incorrect, then both parts of the item are incorrect. For multiple-response items, each correct answer is worth 1 point.

2. To score the writing, refer to the scoring rubric for narrative, opinion/argument, or informative writing. The student's writing is scored with a 4-point scoring rubric. Students may receive 0, 1, 2, 3, or 4 points.

3. In Grade 2, each Performance Task has six questions worth a total of 12 points. After scoring all of the questions, add up the total points to determine a student's score on Part 1.

4. To score the writing in part 2, refer to the scoring rubric for narrative, opinion/argument, or informative writing. The student's writing is scored with a 4-point scoring rubric. Students may receive 0, 1, 2, 3, or 4 points.

The two parts of the task are worth a total of 16 points. For each student, combine the number of points on Part 1 and the number of points on Part 2 to determine a total score. Then refer to the table below to determine an overall rating.

Rating	Score
Excellent	14–16
Good	11–13
Fair	9–10
Needs Improvement	8 or less

Benchmark Advance Interim Assessments and Performance Tasks • © Benchmark Education Company, LLC

Using the Assessment Results

After scoring a Performance Task, review each student's results to see how well he or she performed on each part: the selected-response questions and the writing prompt. Some students will perform well on the first part but not the second, and this information can be valuable in planning further instruction. When scoring the student's responses on two-part items, take note of how many points the student earns for Part A's and how many points for Part B's. This can help you determine what aspect of the task may be challenging for the student.

When reviewing students' responses, you may want to refer to the Common Core State Standards indicated in the Answer Keys to identify areas that require additional instruction.

During standardized reading assessments, students are required to answer different levels of text-dependent comprehension questions. These questions require application of different levels of Webb's Depth of Knowledge—recall, skill/concept, strategic, and extended thinking. Keep these question levels in mind to focus on comprehension development. The questions in each Performance Task provide opportunities for students to rehearse strategies for answering each type of question.

Webb's Depth of Knowledge	
Level of Complexity	**Question Type**
1	**Recall/Reproduction** Recall a fact, information, or procedure; process information on a low level
2	**Skill/Concept** Use information or conceptual knowledge, two or more steps
3	**Strategic Thinking** Requires reasoning, developing a plan or a sequence of steps, more than one reasonable approach
4	**Extended Thinking** Requires connections and extensions, high cognitive demands and complex reasoning

Use the assessment checklist below to evaluate students' use of text-dependent comprehension strategies and provide reteaching opportunities as needed.

Behavior	Always	Sometimes	Not Yet
The student can identify what the question requires him or her to do (for example, locate facts, identify cause and effect, compare and contrast, etc.).			
The student can identify words in the question that will help him or her find the answer in the text.			
The student can find information in the text that answers the question or supports the answer.			
The student can explain the process he or she used to answer the question.			

Based on your assessment of students' performance, use the following tips to revisit and reteach.

1. If the student cannot identify what the question is asking him or her to do . . . Review the comprehension strategies commonly targeted in questions at each level.

2. If the student cannot identify words in the question that will help him or her find the answer in the text . . . Review how to recognize key words in the question for each comprehension strategy.

3. If the student understands what the question is asking but cannot find the answer in the text . . . Model how to skim the text to look for answers or clues and key phrases.

4. If the student can answer the question successfully but cannot explain how he or she came up with the answer . . . Model the steps used to answer the question by creating a steps-in-a-process graphic organizer. Ask the student to retell his or her process using the graphic organizer.

Benchmark Advance Interim Assessments and Performance Tasks • © Benchmark Education Company, LLC

Read the passage aloud as children look at the illustrations on pages 21–22. Then read each question along with the answer choices. Have children circle the correct answer to each question on pages 23–25.

The Man and the Violin

Once upon a time, there lived a poor man. He had only one thing, a violin. The man went to a farm to find work. But the farmer did not need help. The man sat down in a field. He took out his violin and started to play. Soon, the farmer's sheep came to listen. They began to dance. They followed the man when he left.

Next, the man walked through a forest. Some monkeys heard the man playing. They began to dance. The monkeys followed the man.

The man went to the king's gate. Some guards saw the dancing animals. They could not stop laughing.

The king heard the noise. He told the guards to bring the man to his garden. The king saw the dancing animals. He could not stop laughing.

Now, the king had a lovely daughter. But she was always sad. So the king called her to the garden. She saw the man and the dancing animals. For the first time in her life, she laughed and laughed.

The king was so glad. He gave the man half of his kingdom.

continued

Reading Questions

1. Find the picture of the apple. Look at the pictures in the row. Which picture shows a violin? Draw a circle around the picture of a violin.

2. Find the picture of the bell. Look at the pictures in the row. Which person did the man with a violin ask for work? Draw a circle around the picture that shows the person he asked.

3. Find the picture of the truck. Look at the pictures in the row. Which picture shows how the king feels at the end of the story? Circle the picture that shows how the king feels.

4. Find the picture of the pencil. Look at the pictures in the row. Where did the poor man go first: to a forest . . . a farm . . . or a field? Circle the picture that shows where the poor man went first.

5. Find the picture of the boot. Look at the pictures in the row. Where did the poor man go last: to a forest . . . a field . . . or a garden? Circle the picture that shows where the poor man went last.

6. Find the picture of the spoon. Look at the pictures in the row. At the end of the story, who gets half of the kingdom: the guard, the princess, or the poor man? Circle the answer.

7. Find the picture of the banana. Look at the pictures in the row. Which picture shows something that could not happen in real life? Circle the answer.

Read the passage aloud as children look at the illustrations on pages 26–27. Then read each question along with the answer choices. Have children circle the correct answer to each question on pages 28–35.

Giraffes Are Amazing!

Giraffes are the tallest animals. They have long necks. They have long legs. They have small horns on their heads. They are mostly brown and white. Their coats have spots. Every giraffe's coat is different.

How tall are giraffes? They can grow to 18 feet. Their legs are 6 feet long. Even a new baby is tall. It is taller than most people.

Giraffes spend most of the day eating. They even feed at night. They eat plant leaves and buds. They also eat flowers and fruit. Their long necks help them get food. They can reach leaves in tall trees.

Some giraffes fight. They use their necks to hit each other. Giraffes get most of their water from plants. Sometimes they drink water from a pond. First, they spread their legs out wide. Then they lean down to drink. Then they stand up again. It is a funny thing to see.

continued

Reading Questions

8. Find the picture of the chair. Look at the pictures in the row. The passage says that a giraffe's coat has spots. Which picture shows the giraffe's coat? Draw a circle around the picture.

9. Find the picture of the mitten. Look at the pictures in the row. Which picture shows a giraffe's horn? Draw a circle around the picture.

10. Find the picture of the umbrella. Look at the pictures in the row. The passage says that giraffes feed all day. Which picture shows a giraffe feeding? Circle the answer.

11. Find the picture of the apple. Look at the pictures in the row: bugs, meat, leaves. Which picture shows what giraffes eat? Circle the picture.

12. Find the picture of the bell. Look at the pictures in the row: a giraffe spreading its legs, a giraffe running, a giraffe standing up. When a giraffe drinks water, what does it do first? Circle the picture.

13. Find the picture of the truck. Look at the pictures in the row. What part does a giraffe use to fight: its feet . . . horns . . . or neck? Circle the answer.

14. Find the picture of the pencil. Look at the pictures in the row. Which picture shows a bud? Circle the picture of a bud.

15. Find the picture of the boot. Look at the pictures in the row. Why does the author think that giraffes are amazing? Is it because they are so tall . . . they eat a lot . . . or they have spots? Circle the answer.

Reading Foundational Skills Questions

16. Find the picture of the spoon. Look at the letters in the row. Find the letter <u>B</u>. Draw a circle around the letter <u>b</u>.

17. Find the picture of the banana. Look at the letters in the row. Find the letter <u>g</u>. Draw a circle around the letter <u>g</u>.

18. Find the picture of the chair. Look at the letters in the row. Find the letter <u>w</u>. Draw a circle around the letter <u>w</u>.

19. Move down to the next row where you see the picture of a fan. Look at the words. Find the word <u>fan</u>. Draw a circle around the word <u>fan</u>.

20. Move down to the next row where you see the picture of a boy taking a nap. Look at the words. Find the word <u>nap</u>. Draw a circle around the word <u>nap</u>.

21. Move down to the next row where you see the picture of a pit. Look at the words. Find the word <u>pit</u>. Draw a circle around the word <u>pit</u>.

22. Move down to the next row where you see the picture of a mat. Look at the words. Find the word <u>mat</u>. Draw a circle around the word <u>mat</u>.

23. Move down to the next row where you see the picture of a child taking a sip. Look at the words. Find the word <u>sip</u>. Draw a circle around the word <u>sip</u>.

24. Move down to the next row where you see the picture of a map. Look at the words. Find the word <u>map</u>. Draw a circle around the word <u>map</u>.

25. Move down to the next row where you see the picture of a boy named Tim. Look at the words. Find the word <u>Tim</u>. Draw a circle around the word <u>Tim</u>.

continued

Reading Foundational Skills Questions (continued)

26. Move down to the next row where you see the picture of a pin. Look at the words. Find the word <u>pin</u>. Draw a circle around the word <u>pin</u>.

27. Move down to the next row where you see the picture of sap coming from a tree. Look at the words. Find the word <u>sap</u>. Draw a circle around the word <u>sap</u>.

28. Find the picture of the mitten. Look at the words in the row. Listen: That is a big dog. Find the word <u>is</u>. Circle the word <u>is</u>.

29. Find the picture of the umbrella. Look at the words in the row. Listen: He can run fast. Find the word <u>can</u>. Circle the word <u>can</u>.

30. Find the picture of the apple. Look at the words in the row. Listen: I see a turtle. Find the word <u>see</u>. Circle the word <u>see</u>.

Name _____ Date _____

The Man and the Violin

1.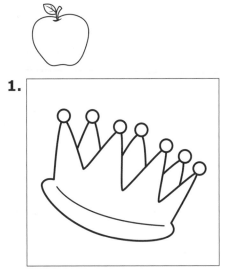

2.

3.

4.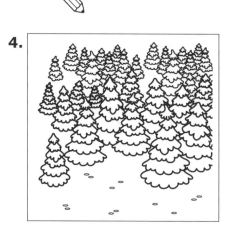

5.

6.

7.

Giraffes Are Amazing!

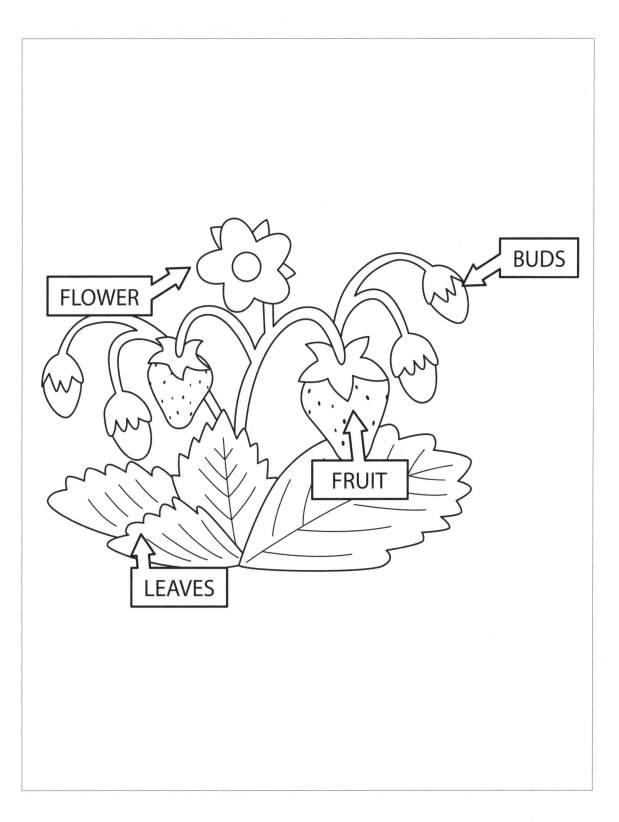

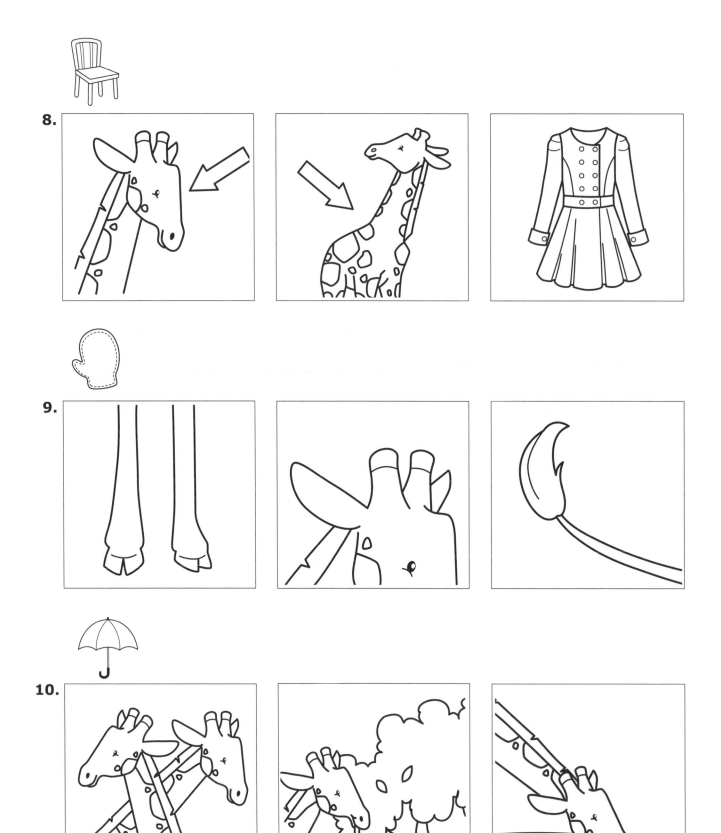

8.

9.

10.

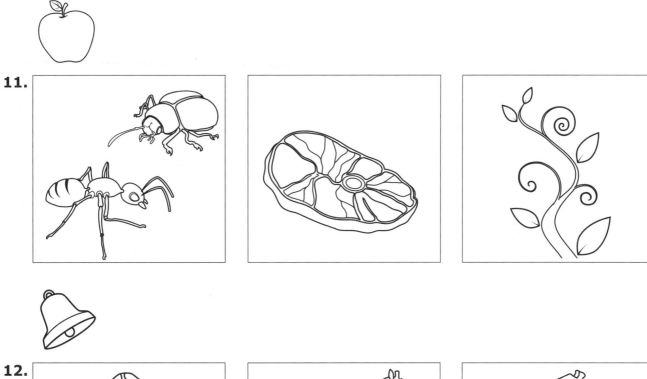

11.

12.

13.

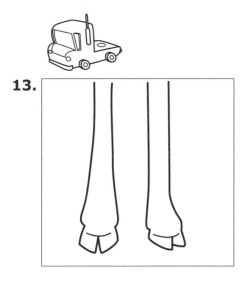 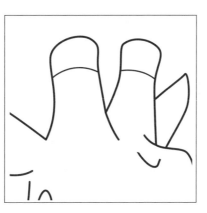 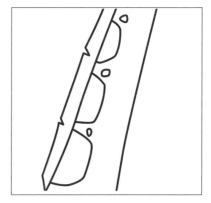

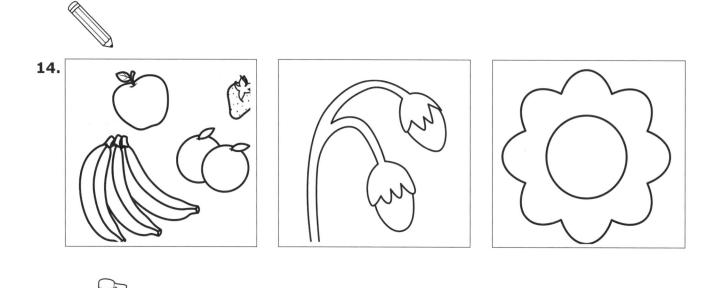

14.

15.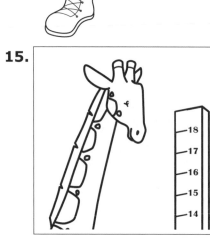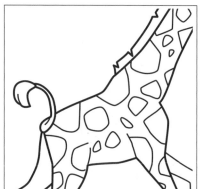

16.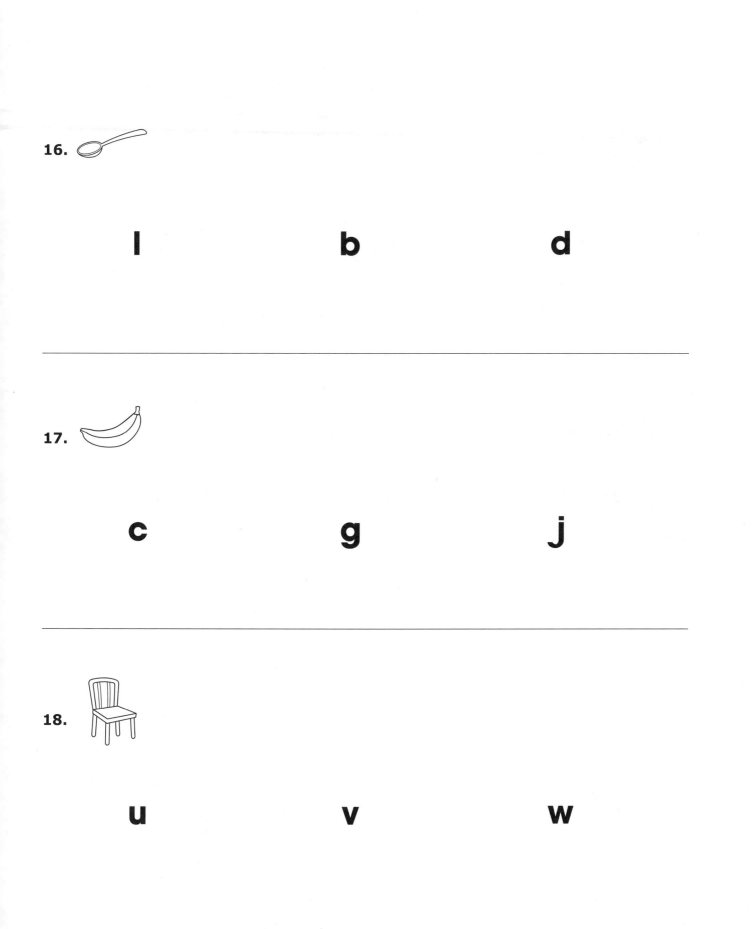

l   b   d

17.

c   g   j

18.

u   v   w

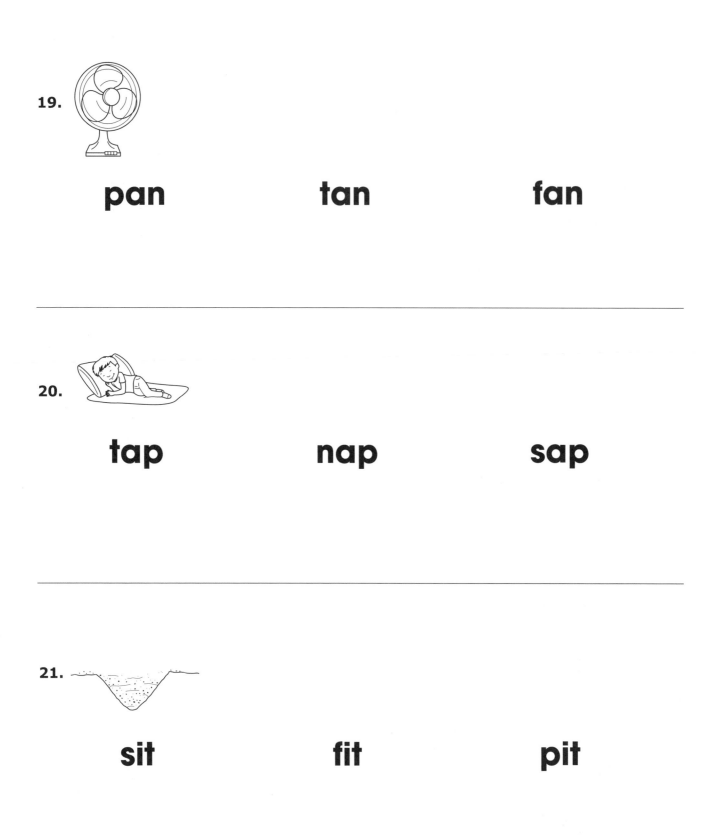

19.

pan   tan   fan

20.

tap   nap   sap

21.

sit   fit   pit

22.

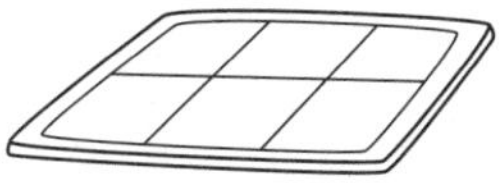

mat   fat   pat

23.

sip   tip   nip

24.

man   map   mat

25.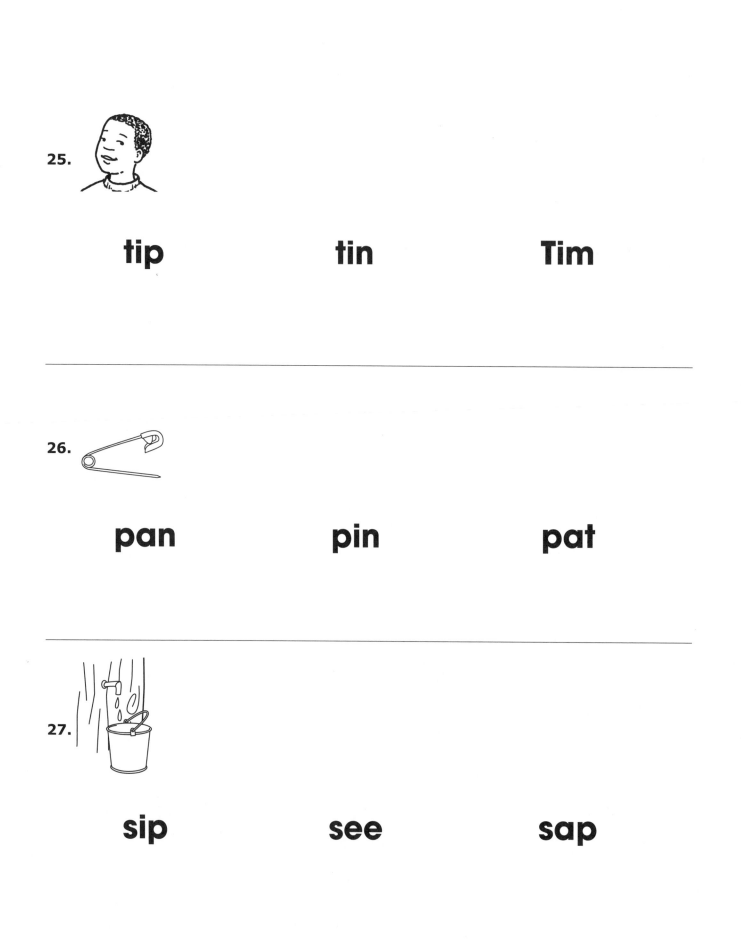

tip   tin   Tim

26.

pan   pin   pat

27.

sip   see   sap

28.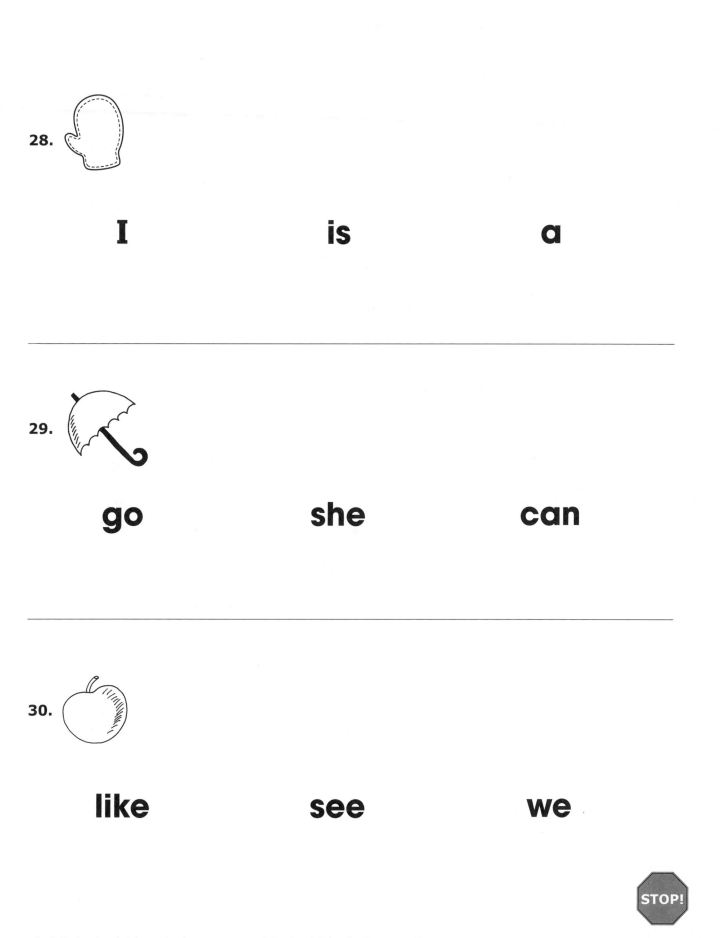

I   is   a

29.

go   she   can

30.

like   see   we

STOP!

Read the passage aloud as children look at the illustrations on pages 41–42. Then read each question along with the answer choices. Have children circle the correct answer to each question on pages 43–45.

A Mouse in Winter

It was a hot, sunny morning. But Mouse knew that winter was coming. She needed a warm place to live.

Mouse started working right away. She spotted some branches. They were heavy. Then Mouse saw her friend, Rabbit.

"Rabbit, I'm building a house for winter. Can you help me?"

"Silly Mouse," Rabbit said. "It's a warm day. I'm busy reading my book."

Then Mouse saw Bear. He was large and strong.

"Bear, I'm building a house for winter. Can you help me?"

"Silly Mouse," Bear said. "It is summer, not winter."

Mouse felt sad, but she kept working.

Mouse finished the house just in time. Cold winds blew, and snow started to fall. Then she heard a knock on her door. It was Rabbit and Bear.

"Please let us in! We have no place to go," they said.

Mouse let Rabbit and Bear stay. It was very crowded. But they all stayed warm.

Reading Questions

1. Find the picture of the apple. Look at the pictures in the row. What is Rabbit doing when Mouse first sees him? Is Rabbit reading a book . . . building a house . . . or eating lettuce? Draw a circle around the picture that shows what Rabbit is doing.

2. Find the picture of the bell. The story says the branches are heavy. Look at the pictures in the row. Which picture shows something that is heavy? Draw a circle around the picture that shows something heavy.

3. Find the picture of the truck. The story says Mouse spotted some branches. Look at the pictures in the row. Which picture shows what the word <u>spotted</u> means in this story? Circle the picture that shows what <u>spotted</u> means.

4. Find the picture of the pencil. Look at the pictures in the row. In the story, why is Mouse sad? Is Mouse sad because she has to cook dinner . . . because her friends will not help her . . . or because it is snowing outside? Circle the answer.

5. Find the picture of the boot. The story says Bear is large. Look at the words in the row: <u>big</u> . . . <u>little</u> . . . <u>fun</u>. Which word means the opposite of <u>large</u>? Circle the word.

6. Find the picture of the spoon. Look at the pictures in the row. Which picture shows what happens at the end of the story? Circle the answer.

7. Find the picture of the banana. Look at the pictures in the row. What will Rabbit and Bear probably do next year before winter starts? Will they go to school . . . climb a tree . . . or build a house? Circle the answer.

8. Find the picture of the chair. Look at the pictures in the row. What lesson does this story teach you? Does it teach you to share your toys . . . help your friends . . . or try your best? Circle the answer.

continued ▶

Read the passage aloud as children look at the illustrations on pages 46–47. Then read each question along with the answer choices. Have children circle the correct answer to each question on pages 48–55.

Sneakers

Do you have a pair of sneakers? Many people do. Sneakers have been around for a long time.

The first sneakers did not look like sneakers do today. They were like shoes. They had a piece of rubber on the bottom. Rubber is used to make tires.

Then sneakers got better. At first, people only wore them to play sports. They were called "sports shoes." Then kids wore them all the time. They were called "sneakers" because they were quiet. A person with sneakers could sneak up on you.

Today, sneakers come in many colors. Some kinds of sneakers are special. The soles are filled with air or gel. They help people jump higher or run faster. Kids even have sneakers that light up! Those are fun.

Reading Questions

9. Find the picture of the mitten. Look at the pictures in the row. What is something made from rubber? Is it a hat . . . a tire . . . or a fence? Circle the picture.

10. Find the picture of the umbrella. The passage says sneakers are quiet. Look at the pictures in the row. Which picture shows what <u>quiet</u> means? Circle the picture that shows what <u>quiet</u> means.

11. Find the picture of the apple. Look at the pictures in the row. Why did people first wear sneakers? Was it to go to school . . . to play sports . . . or to work outside? Circle the answer.

12. Find the picture of the bell. Look at the pictures in the row. Where is the sole of the sneaker? Circle the picture that shows the sole.

13. Find the picture of the truck. Look at the pictures in the row. In the second picture that goes with the passage, what do sneakers help the basketball player do? Do they help him climb . . . walk . . . or jump? Circle the answer.

14. Find the picture of the pencil. Look at the pictures in the row. The author says that some sneakers light up. Does this tell you how sneakers look . . . feel . . . or sound? Circle the answer.

15. Find the picture of the boot. Why does the author think some sneakers are special? Look at the pictures in the row. Is it because they help people make friends . . . run fast . . . or sneak up on others? Circle the answer.

continued

Reading Foundational Skills Questions

16. Find the picture of the spoon. Look at the words in the row: <u>bat</u>, <u>bats</u>, <u>bit</u>. Which word's ending means "more than one"? Draw a circle around the word.

17. Find the picture of the banana. Listen: You can jump higher. Find the word <u>jump</u>. Draw a circle around the word <u>jump</u>.

18. Find the picture of the chair. Look at the words in the row. Find the word <u>cat</u> . . . <u>cat</u>. Circle the word.

19. Find the picture of the mitten. Look at the words in the row. Find the word <u>rub</u> . . . <u>rub</u>. Circle the word.

20. Find the picture of the umbrella. Listen: A dog has four legs. Find the word <u>has</u>. Circle the word <u>has</u>.

21. Find the picture of the apple. Look at the words in the row. Find the word <u>log</u> . . . <u>log</u>. Circle the word.

22. Find the picture of the bell. Look at the words in the row. Find the word <u>him</u> . . . <u>him</u>. Circle the word.

23. Find the picture of the truck. Look at the words in the row. Find the word <u>red</u> . . . <u>red</u>. Circle the word.

24. Find the picture of the pencil. Listen: A paper is on the desk. Find the word <u>the</u>. Circle the word <u>the</u>.

25. Find the picture of the boot. Look at the words in the row. Which word begins with the same sound as <u>call</u> . . . <u>call</u>? Circle the word.

26. Find the picture of the spoon. Look at the words in the row. Which word begins with the same sound as <u>get</u> . . . <u>get</u>? Circle the word.

27. Find the picture of the banana. Look at the words in the row. Which word begins with the same sound as <u>fill</u> . . . <u>fill</u>? Circle the word.

28. Find the picture of the chair. Look at the words in the row. Which word ends with the same sound as <u>met</u> . . . <u>met</u>? Circle the word.

29. Find the picture of the mitten. Look at the words in the row. Which word ends with the same sound as <u>bed</u> . . . <u>bed</u>? Circle the word.

30. Find the picture of the umbrella. Listen: She goes to school. Find the word <u>she</u>. Circle the word <u>she</u>.

Name _____ Date _____

A Mouse in Winter

1.

2.

3.

4.

5.

big	little	fun

6.

7.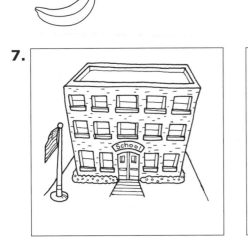

8.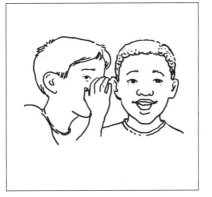

Sneakers

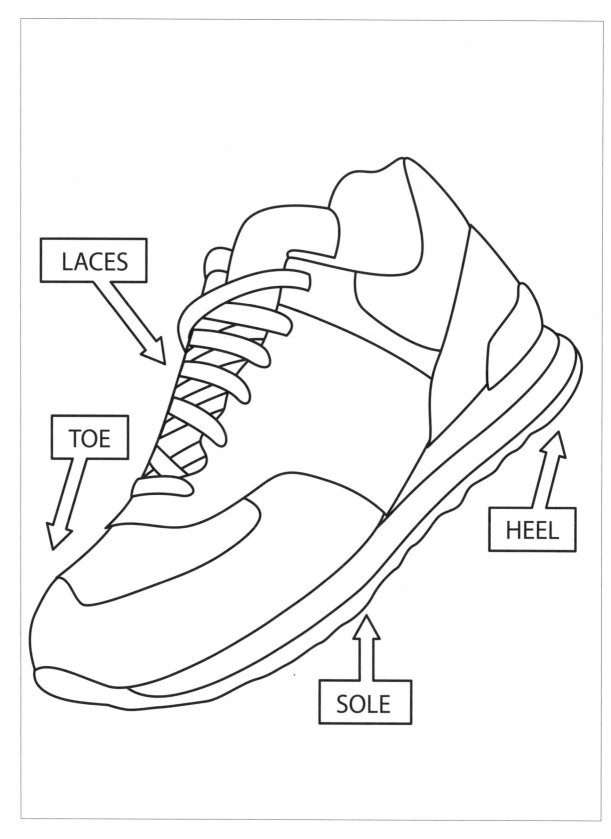

LACES

TOE

HEEL

SOLE

9.

10.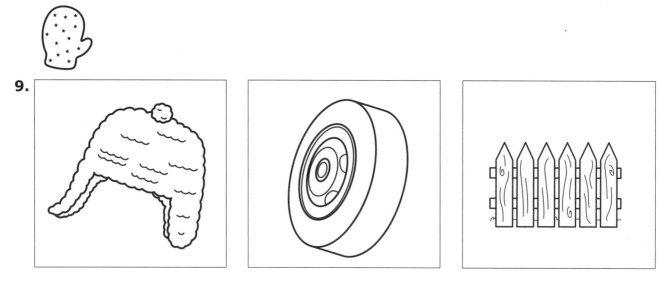

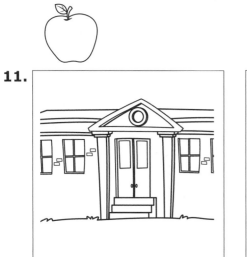

11.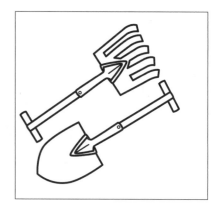

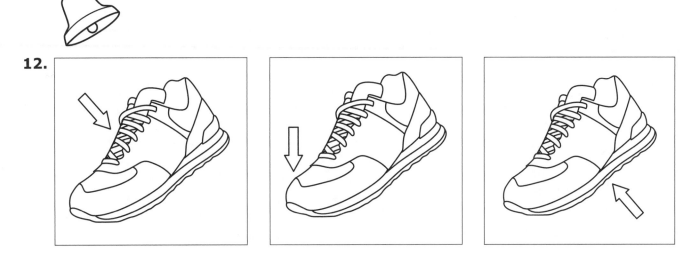

12.

13.

14.

15.

16.

bat   **bats**   **bit**

17.

jam   **jump**   **get**

18.

cut   **cot**   **cat**

19.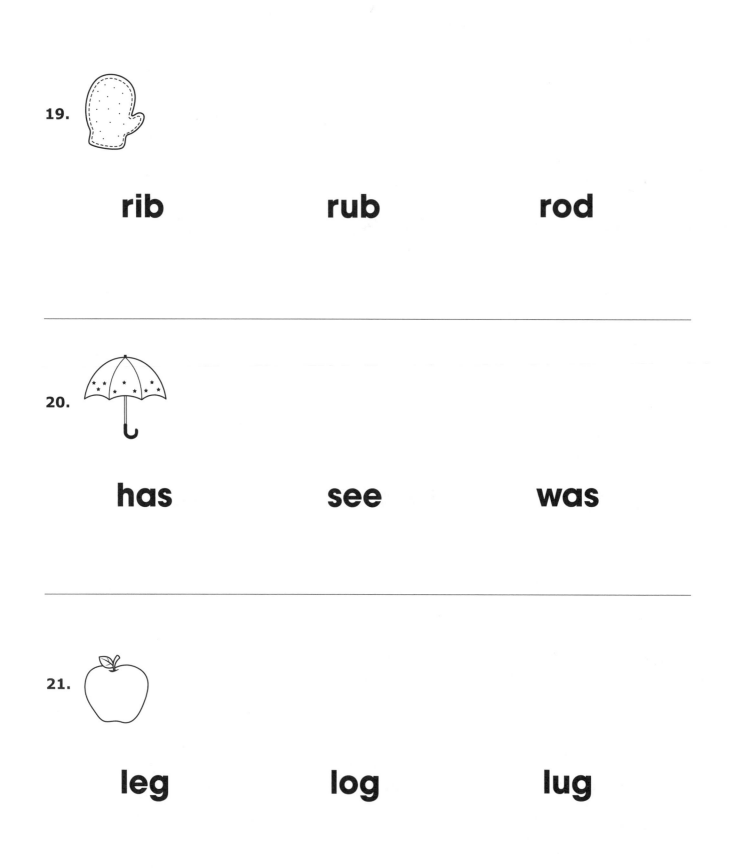

rib   rub   rod

20.

has   see   was

21.

leg   log   lug

22.

him   hum   ham

23.

rid   red   rod

24.

we   the   ten

25.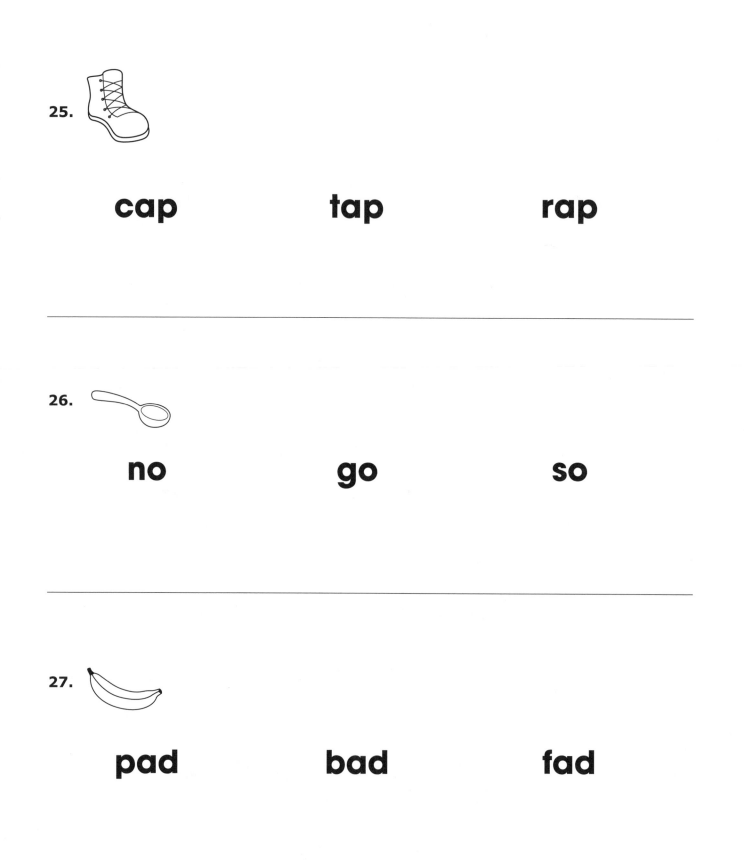

cap　　　　　**tap**　　　　　**rap**

26.

no　　　　　**go**　　　　　**so**

27.

pad　　　　　**bad**　　　　　**fad**

28.

hog hot hop

29.

sap sad sat

30.

she see he

Read the passage aloud as children look at the illustrations on pages 61–62. Then read each question along with the answer choices. Have children circle the correct answer to each question on pages 63–65.

The Cobbler and the Elves

Once there was a poor cobbler. He worked hard making shoes. But people did not buy them. Things got worse. Finally, he had only enough leather for one last pair of shoes. The cobbler went to bed. He would make the shoes tomorrow.

Next morning, the shoes were already made! "How did that happen?" the cobbler wondered. Just then, a woman came in. The shoes were just what she wanted. She gave the cobbler money. He used it to get more leather.

That night, the same thing happened. This time, three pairs of shoes were made.

This went on day after day. Who was making the shoes? To find out, the cobbler hid and watched. Late that night, two elves came. In no time at all, they made all the leather into shoes. Then they slipped away like mice.

The cobbler wanted to help the elves. He said to his wife, "The elves have old rags for clothes. Can you make some new ones for them?"

The elves loved their new suits. They put the suits on. Then they danced out the door. The cobbler never saw them again. But because of their help, he was never poor again.

Reading Questions

1. Find the picture of the apple. Look at the pictures in the row. A cobbler is a person who makes what: clothes . . . beds . . . or shoes? Draw a circle around the picture that shows what a cobbler makes.

2. Find the picture of the bell. Look at the pictures in the row. How did the cobbler feel when he found the first pair of shoes? Did he feel scared . . . surprised . . . or angry? Circle the picture that shows how the cobbler felt.

3. Find the picture of the truck. Look at the sentences. The second picture that goes with the story shows an elf. What does the picture tell you about the elf? Circle the answer.

4. Find the picture of the pencil. Look at the pictures in the row. Who made new clothes for the elves? Was it an elf . . . the cobbler . . . or the cobbler's wife? Circle the picture that shows who made the new clothes.

5. Find the picture of the boot. Look at the pictures in the row. Which picture shows what happened at the end of the story? Circle the picture.

6. Find the picture of the spoon. Look at the pictures in the row. What part of the story could not happen in real life? Circle the picture.

7. Find the picture of the banana. Look at the pictures in the row: mice . . . door . . . and money. Which belongs in a group of words named "Parts of a House"? Circle the picture.

continued

Read the passage aloud as children look at the illustrations on pages 66–67. Then read each question along with the answer choices. Have children circle the correct answer to each question on pages 68–75.

Neighbors Build a Playground

People near Oak Street wanted a place for children to play. They asked about using an empty piece of land. The city said yes. They could use it. But the empty lot was not safe. It was full of trash. The first thing to do was clean it up. Both kids and grownups helped.

The next step was to make the ground flat and even. A bulldozer came and did that work.

Finally, the space was ready. Kids told the grownups what they liked to do. The grownups built a big wooden castle. It had places to climb and hide. They put in a slide. And they left plenty of room for running around.

The kids helped with the work. They painted. They handed tools to the grownups. They picked up nails so no one would step on them.

The new playground is now open. Anyone from the city can use it. Every day it is filled with kids.

Reading Questions

8. Find the picture of the chair. Look at the pictures in the row. Which picture shows what happened first? Circle the picture that shows what happened first.

9. Find the picture of the mitten. Look at the pictures in the row. The passage says the kids helped by handing something to the grownups who were working. Which picture shows what the kids handed to the adults? Circle the picture.

10. Find the picture of the umbrella. Look at the pictures in the row. What did the people use to make the ground flat and even: a shovel . . . a dump truck . . . or a bulldozer? Circle the picture.

11. Find the picture of the apple. Look at the pictures in the row. What did both the grownups and the kids do together? Did they pick up trash, run a race, or cut pieces of wood? Circle the answer.

12. Find the picture of the bell. Look at the sentences. Now, look at the second picture that goes with the passage. What would be a good caption for this picture? Circle the answer.

13. Find the picture of the truck. Look at the pictures in the row. The passage uses the word <u>trash</u>. Which picture shows some trash? Circle the picture.

14. Find the picture of the pencil. The passage says the empty lot was not safe. Which picture shows what the word <u>lot</u> means in this passage? Circle the picture.

15. Find the picture of the boot. Look at the pictures in the row. The author wrote this passage to tell about what: a castle . . . a playground . . . or tools? Circle the answer.

continued

Reading Foundational Skills Questions

16. Find the picture of the spoon. Look at the words in the row. Find the word <u>bed</u> . . . <u>bed</u>. Circle the word.

17. Find the picture of the banana. Look at the words in the row. Find the word <u>rid</u> . . . <u>rid</u>. Circle the word.

18. Find the picture of the chair. Look at the words in the row. Find the word <u>get</u> . . . <u>get</u>. Circle the word.

19. Find the picture of the mitten. Look at the words in the row. Find the word <u>made</u> . . . <u>made</u>. Circle the word.

20. Find the picture of the umbrella. Look at the words in the row. Find the word <u>hid</u> . . . <u>hid</u>. Circle the word.

21. Find the picture of the apple. Look at the words in the row. Find the word <u>hop</u> . . . <u>hop</u>. Circle the word.

22. Find the picture of the bell. Look at the words in the row. Find the word <u>Cam</u> . . . <u>Cam</u>. Circle the word.

23. Find the picture of the truck. Look at the words in the row. Find the word that ends with the same sound as the word <u>cat</u> . . . <u>cat</u>. Circle the word.

24. Find the picture of the pencil. Look at the words in the row. Find the word that has the same vowel sound as the word <u>nice</u> . . . <u>nice</u>. Circle the word.

25. Find the picture of the boot. Look at the words in the row. Find the word that has the same vowel sound as the word <u>run</u> . . . <u>run</u>. Circle the word.

26. Find the picture of the spoon. Look at the words in the row. Which word has an ending that means "more than one"? Circle the word.

27. Find the picture of the banana. Look at the words in the row. Which word has an ending that means "more than one"? Circle the word.

28. Find the picture of the chair. Look at the words in the row. Listen: He has big feet. Find the word <u>big</u> . . . <u>big</u>. Circle the word.

29. Find the picture of the mitten. Look at the words in the row. Listen: He doesn't know what to do. Find the word <u>what</u> . . . <u>what</u>. Circle the word.

30. Find the picture of the umbrella. Look at the words in the row. Listen: She said goodbye to me. Find the word <u>said</u> . . . <u>said</u>. Circle the word.

The Cobbler and the Elves

1.

2.

3.

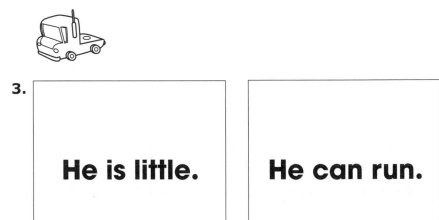

| He is little. | He can run. | He is rich. |

4.

5.

6.

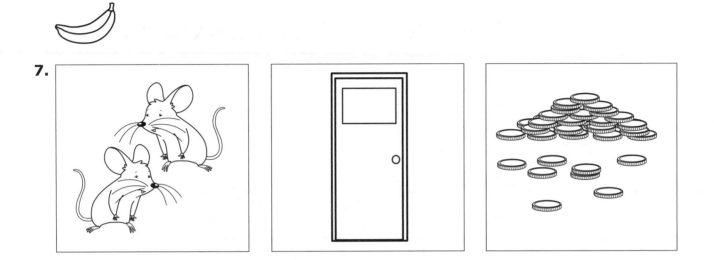

7.

Neighbors Build a Playground

8.

9.

10.

11.

12.

| Kids can play here. | Big and little kids had jobs. | He has a hat. |

13.

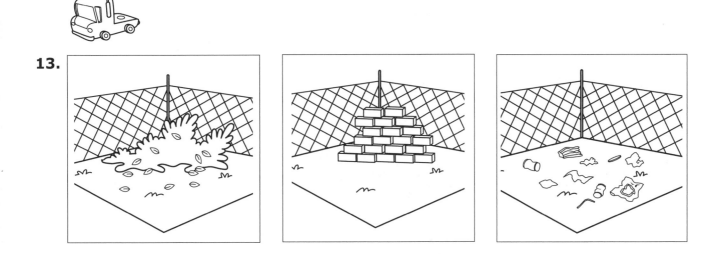

14.

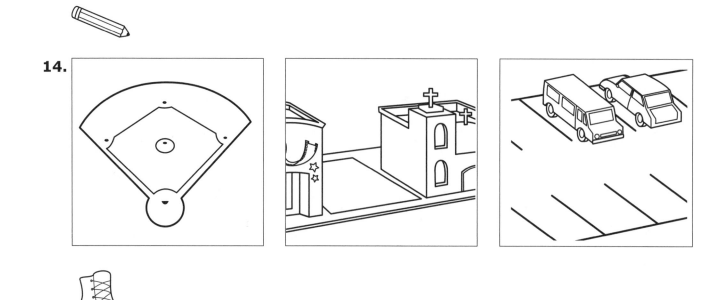

15.

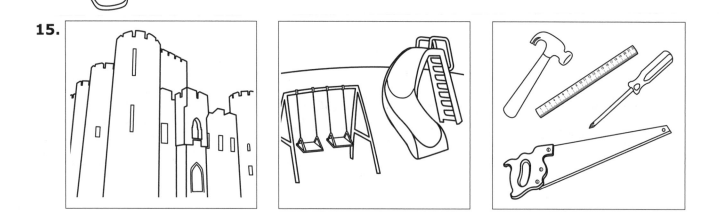

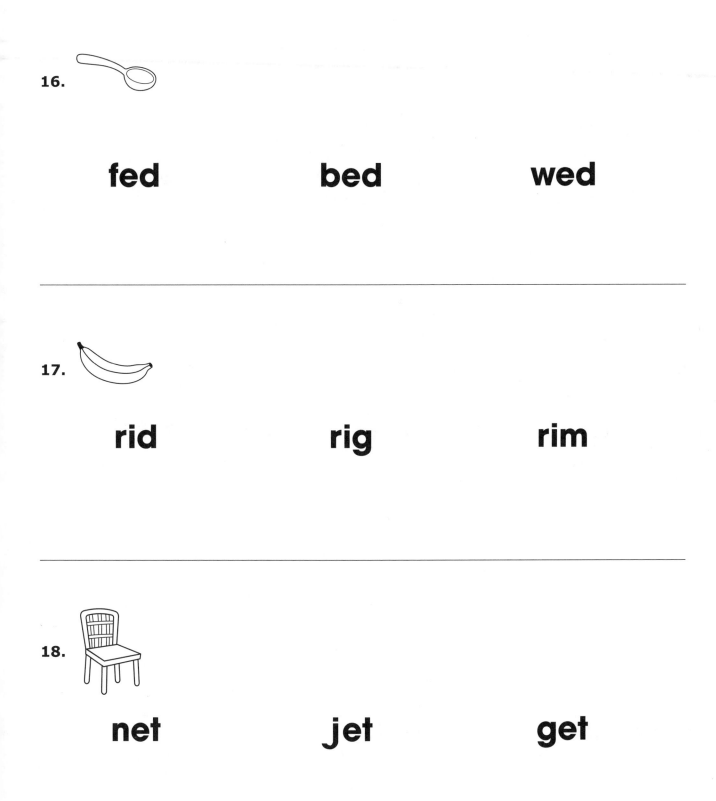

16.

fed   bed   wed

17.

rid   rig   rim

18.

net   jet   get

19.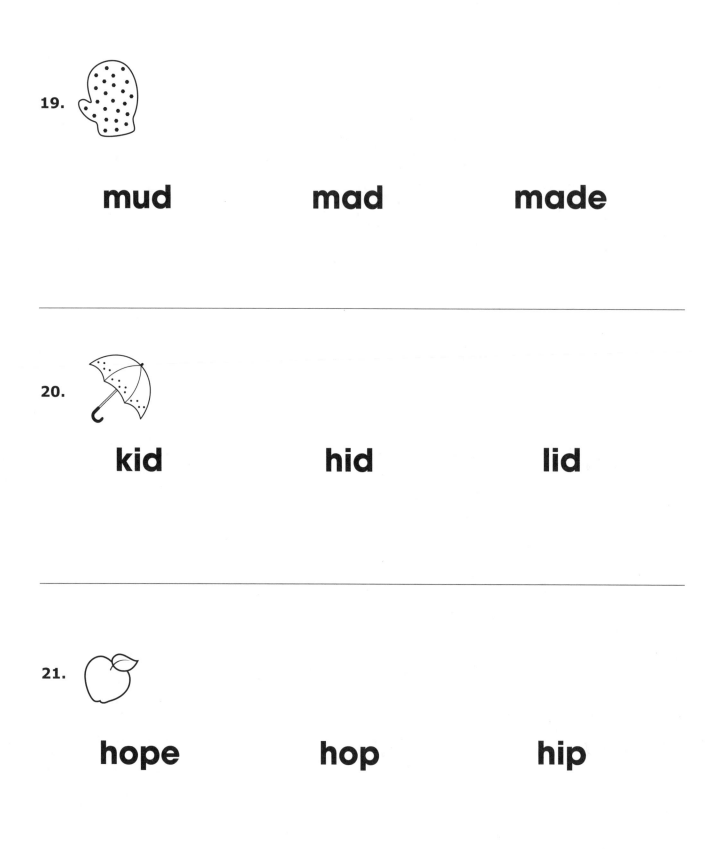

mud   mad   made

20.

kid   hid   lid

21.

hope   hop   hip

22.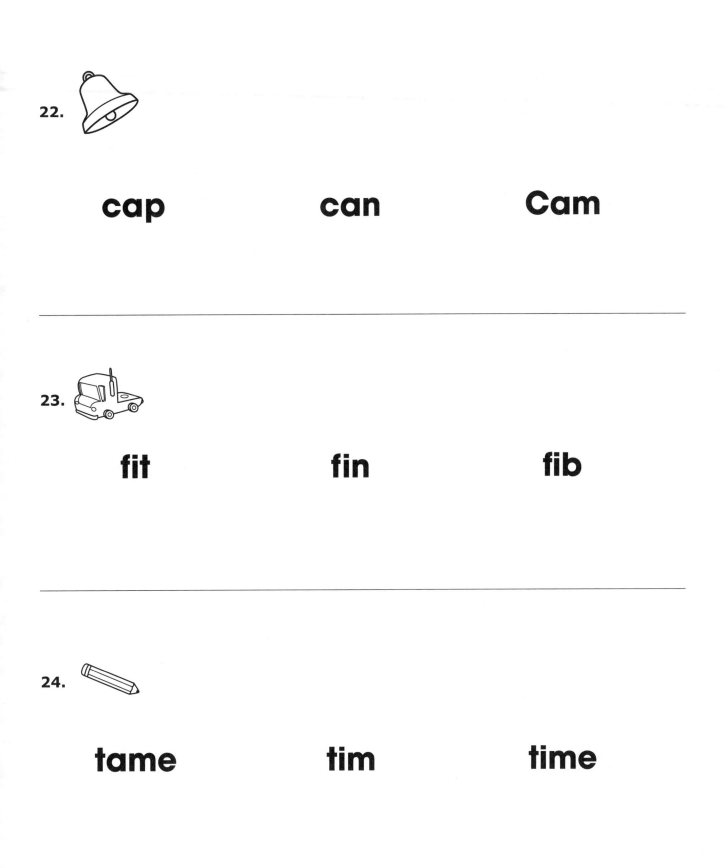

cap   can   Cam

23.

fit   fin   fib

24.

tame   tim   time

25.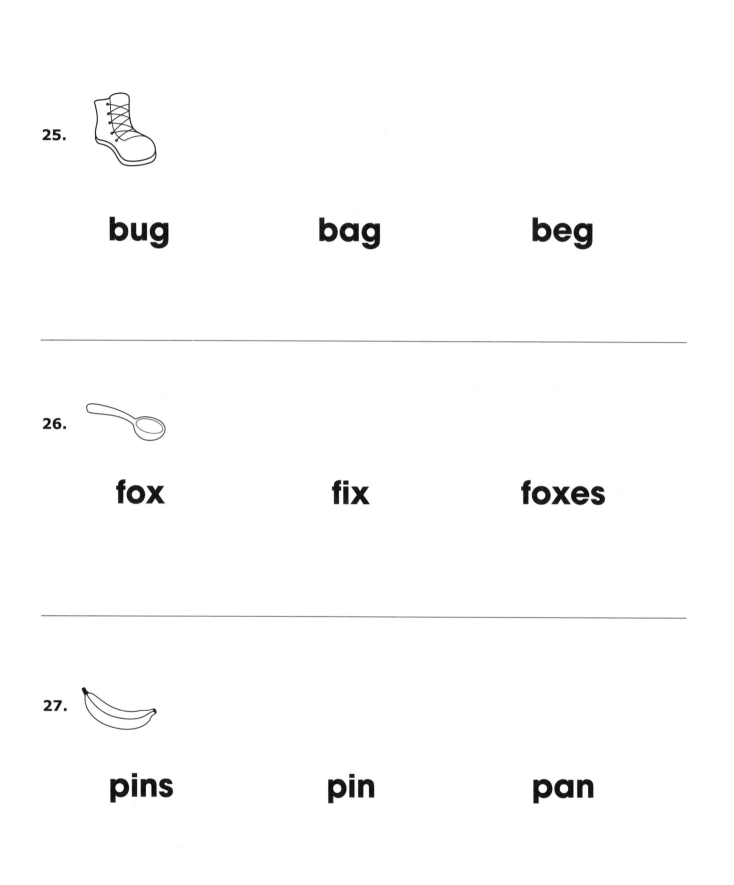

bug **bag** **beg**

26.

fox **fix** **foxes**

27.

pins **pin** **pan**

28.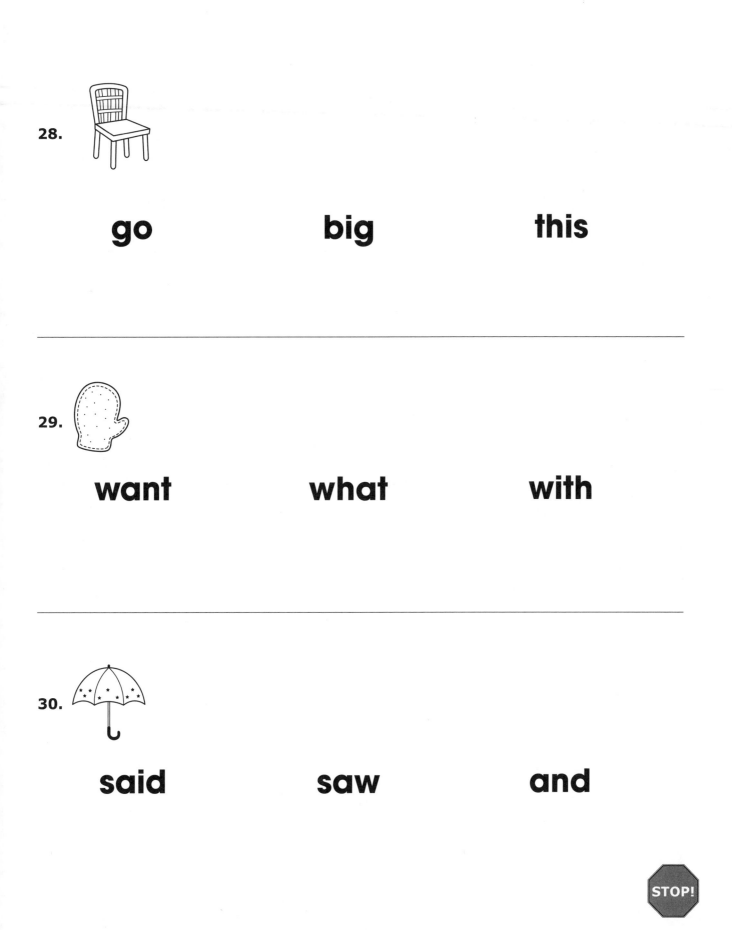

go   big   this

29.

want   what   with

30.

said   saw   and

STOP!

Grade K Interim Assessments Answer Keys

Interim Assessment 1

Question	Answer	Standard Assessed
1.	2nd picture (violin)	RL.K.4, L.K.4, L.K.6
2.	3rd picture (farmer)	RL.K.4, L.K.4, L.K.6
3.	1st picture (king smiling)	RL.K.3
4.	2nd picture (farm)	RL.K.3
5.	3rd picture (garden)	RL.K.3
6.	3rd picture (poor man)	RL.K.1, RL.K.2
7.	2nd picture (animals dancing)	RL.K.5, RL.K.7
8.	2nd picture (coat)	RI.K.4, L.K.4, L.K.6
9.	2nd picture (horns)	RI.K.4, L.K.4, L.K.6
10.	2nd picture (feed)	RI.K.4, L.K.4, L.K.6
11.	3rd picture (leaves)	RI.K.1, RI.K.2
12.	1st picture (legs spread)	RI.K.3
13.	3rd picture (neck)	RI.K.1, RI.K.2
14.	2nd picture (bud)	RI.K.7
15.	1st picture (so tall)	RI.K.8
16.	b	RF.K.3a
17.	g	RF.K.3a
18.	w	RF.K.3a
19.	fan	L.K.2d, Initial f
20.	nap	L.K.2d, Initial n
21.	pit	L.K.2d, Initial p
22.	mat	L.K.2d, Initial m
23.	sip	L.K.2d, Initial s
24.	map	L.K.2d, Final p
25.	Tim	L.K.2d, Final m
26.	pin	L.K.2d, Short i
27.	sap	L.K.2d, Short a
28.	is	RF.K.3c
29.	can	RF.K.3c
30.	see	RF.K.3c

Interim Assessment 2

Question	Answer	Standard Assessed
1.	1st picture (reading a book)	RL.K.1, RL.K.2
2.	3rd picture (barbell)	RL.K.4, L.K.5b, L.K.6
3.	2nd picture (pointing to bird)	L.K.4a, L.K.6
4.	2nd picture (friends not helping)	RL.K.3
5.	little	RL.K.4, L.K.5b, L.K.6
6.	1st picture (animals in bed)	RL.K.3
7.	3rd picture (build a house)	RL.K.1
8.	2nd picture (help your friends)	RL.K.2
9.	2nd picture (tire)	RI.K.1
10.	1st picture (quiet)	RI.K.4, L.K.4, L.K.6
11.	2nd picture (to play sports)	RI.K.3
12.	3rd picture (sole)	RI.K.1, RI.K.7
13.	3rd picture (jump)	RI.K.7
14.	1st picture (look)	L.K.5a, L.K.6
15.	2nd picture (run fast)	RI.K.8
16.	bats	L.K.2d, Plural with -s
17.	jump	RF.K.3c, HFW
18.	cat	L.K.2d, Short a
19.	rub	L.K.2d, Short u
20.	has	RF.K.3c, HFW
21.	log	L.K.2d, Short o
22.	him	L.K.2d, Short i
23.	red	L.K.2d, Short e
24.	the	RF.K.3c, HFW
25.	cap	L.K.2d, Initial c
26.	go	L.K.2d, Initial g
27.	fad	L.K.2d, Initial f
28.	hot	L.K.2d, Final t
29.	sad	L.K.2d, Final d
30.	she	RF.K.3c, HFW

Interim Assessment 3

Question	Answer	Standard Assessed
1.	3rd picture (shoes)	RL.K.4
2.	2nd picture (surprise)	RL.K.3
3.	He is little.	RL.K.7
4.	3rd picture (cobbler's wife)	RL.K.1, RL.K.2
5.	2nd picture (elves leaving)	RL.K.3
6.	2nd picture (elf with thread)	RL.K.5
7.	2nd picture (door)	L.K.5a
8.	2nd picture (pick up trash)	RI.K.3
9.	1st picture (tool)	RI.K.1, RI.K.2
10.	3rd picture (bulldozer)	RI.K.3
11.	1st picture (cleaned up trash)	RI.K.5
12.	Kids can play here.	RI.K.5
13.	3rd picture (trash)	RI.K.4, L.K.5c, L.K.6
14.	2nd picture (empty lot)	RI.K.4, L.K.4a
15.	2nd picture (playground)	RI.K.8
16.	bed	L.K.2d, Initial b
17.	rid	L.K.2d, Final d
18.	get	L.K.2d, Initial g
19.	made	L.K.2d, Long a, a_e
20.	hid	L.K.2d, Initial h
21.	hop	L.K.2d, Short o
22.	Cam	L.K.2d, Final m
23.	fit	L.K.2d, Final t
24.	time	L.K.2d, Long i, i_e
25.	bug	L.K.2d, Short u
26.	foxes	L.K.2d, Plural with -es
27.	pins	L.K.2d, Plural with -s
28.	big	RF.K.3c, HFW
29.	what	RF.K.3c, HFW
30.	said	RF.K.3c, HFW

Interim Assessment Progress Class Chart

Directions: Record scores for each student on each assessment.

Student	Interim Assessment 1 (Pretest)	Assessment 2	Assessment 3	Interim Assessment 1 (Posttest)

Grade K Interim Assessment 1
Scoring Chart (Pretest / Posttest)

Teacher Name _____ Date _____

Student Name _____

Directions: For Reading and Reading Foundational Skills, place a check mark (✓) above the item number for each correct answer. To find the total score, add the number of check marks.

Reading (Item Numbers)				
1	2	3	4	5
6	7	8	9	10
11	12	13	14	15

Reading Foundational Skills				
16	17	18	19	20
21	22	23	24	25
26	27	28	29	30

Total Score (Number of points ÷ 30 × 100 = %)	**/30**	**%**

Comments

Grade K Interim Assessment 2 Scoring Chart

Teacher Name _____   Date _____

Student Name _____

Directions: For Reading and Reading Foundational Skills, place a check mark (✓) above the item number for each correct answer. To find the total score, add the number of check marks.

Reading (Item Numbers)				
1	2	3	4	5
6	7	8	9	10
11	12	13	14	15

Reading Foundational Skills				
16	17	18	19	20
21	22	23	24	25
26	27	28	29	30

Total Score (Number of points ÷ 30 × 100 = %)	/30	%
Comments		

Grade K Interim Assessment 3 Scoring Chart

Teacher Name _____   Date _____

Student Name _____

Directions: For Reading and Reading Foundational Skills, place a check mark (✓) above the item number for each correct answer. To find the total score, add the number of check marks.

Reading (Item Numbers)				
1	2	3	4	5
6	7	8	9	10
11	12	13	14	15

Reading Foundational Skills				
16	17	18	19	20
21	22	23	24	25
26	27	28	29	30

Total Score (Number of points ÷ 30 × 100 = %)	**/30**	**%**
Comments		